Peter Ngibuini Kuguru HSC

Factors Affecting the Performance of Coffee Industry in Kenya

Peter Ngibuini Kuguru HSC

Factors Affecting the Performance of Coffee Industry in Kenya

LAP LAMBERT Academic Publishing

Impressum / Imprint

Bibliografische Information der Deutschen Nationalbibliothek: Die Deutsche Nationalbibliothek verzeichnet diese Publikation in der Deutschen Nationalbibliografie; detaillierte bibliografische Daten sind im Internet über http://dnb.d-nb.de abrufbar.

Alle in diesem Buch genannten Marken und Produktnamen unterliegen warenzeichen-, marken- oder patentrechtlichem Schutz bzw. sind Warenzeichen oder eingetragene Warenzeichen der jeweiligen Inhaber. Die Wiedergabe von Marken, Produktnamen, Gebrauchsnamen, Handelsnamen, Warenbezeichnungen u.s.w. in diesem Werk berechtigt auch ohne besondere Kennzeichnung nicht zu der Annahme, dass solche Namen im Sinne der Warenzeichen- und Markenschutzgesetzgebung als frei zu betrachten wären und daher von jedermann benutzt werden dürften.

Bibliographic information published by the Deutsche Nationalbibliothek: The Deutsche Nationalbibliothek lists this publication in the Deutsche Nationalbibliografie; detailed bibliographic data are available in the Internet at http://dnb.d-nb.de.

Any brand names and product names mentioned in this book are subject to trademark, brand or patent protection and are trademarks or registered trademarks of their respective holders. The use of brand names, product names, common names, trade names, product descriptions etc. even without a particular marking in this work is in no way to be construed to mean that such names may be regarded as unrestricted in respect of trademark and brand protection legislation and could thus be used by anyone.

Coverbild / Cover image: www.ingimage.com

Verlag / Publisher:
LAP LAMBERT Academic Publishing
ist ein Imprint der / is a trademark of
OmniScriptum GmbH & Co. KG
Bahnhofstraße 28, 66111 Saarbrücken, Deutschland / Germany
Email: info@lap-publishing.com

Herstellung: siehe letzte Seite /
Printed at: see last page
ISBN: 978-3-659-56138-2

Zugl. / Approved by: Nairobi, Management University of Africa, 2015

FACTORS AFFECTING THE PERFORMANCE OF COFFEE INDUSTRY IN KENYA

PETER NGIBUINI KUGURU HSC

ACKNOWLEDGEMENT

I would like to thank my advisor Dr. Kennedy Ogollah and my supervisor, David Kanyanjua who provided detailed guidance and encouragement throughout the course of preparing this study and conducting the research. They were kind to accept my calls at odd hours and even when they could not accept my calls he called me back and responded to all my questions.

My thanks go to my classmates for their positive attitude and comrade support. They shared their time and ideas.

My special acknowledgement to my office support staff Ms. Anne Katua and Mr. Fredrick Kakui for their organizational role and support.

ABSTRACT

This study sought to determine the factors affecting the performance of the coffee indusrtry in Kenya with a case study of Mathira Constituency. The study sought to find the existing linear relationship between the factors affecting the coffee industry and performance of the coffee industry. The factors that were considered included quality of coffee, growers capacity, government policies and marketing factors. The study was grounded on public interest theory of regulation, total quality management theory and Theory of Performance.

Mixed mode research approach was used which consisted of the descriptive research design and correlation research design. Simple random sampling technique was used and the sample consisted of 385 respondents out of a population of 26,000 farmers. The study involved a primary data collection from the coffee farmers and the coffee cooperative society managers. The collected data was edited, coded, keyed in and analyzed using Statistical Package for Social Sciences (SPSS). The study findings showed that all the factors have a positive significant relationship with the performance of coffee industry in Kenya. The factor combined accounted for 28% of the performance of coffee industry.

Quality of coffee had a significantly positive relationship with the performance of coffee industry in Kenya. From the regression analysis the study obtained a beta coefficient of 0.155 which suggests a positive and significant relation between the two variables. Grower's capacity has a positive significant effect on coffee industry performance in Kenya. Government policy also had a positive significant effect on the performance of coffee industry in Kenya as well as marketing process. The study will benefit the farming community in the coffee industry, the cooperative movement, the marketers, the government, the interested publics in the performance of coffee industry and the population of Kenya.

Based on the findings above the study concluded that quality of coffee produced, grower's capacity, government policies and marketing process are significantly related to performance of coffee industry in Kenya. The study therefore recommends that CBK, government of Kenya, donors, coffee farmers in Kenya and others policy makers should adopt this study finding in order to raise the performance of coffee industry in Kenya.

TABLE OF CONTENTS

LIST OF FIGURES

LIST OF TABLES

CHAPTER ONE

INTRODUCTION

This section presents the background to the study, problem statement, research objectives, and research questions, scope of the study, justification of the study, significance of the study, limitations of the study and area of the study and organization of the study.

Background to the study

Performance of the coffee sector has been attributed to the ration of farm price to auction price (Lilieholm, 2010). Brazil in particular has higher ratio of farm price to auction price than most sub-Saharan countries in Africa due to supportive government policies, large number of skilled coffee growers as well as high level of technology (Ojambo, 2013). However, Nathalie (2002) indicates that although government policies in Brazil are supportive, the quality of coffee in Brazil is relatively lower than that of Columbia, Ethiopia and Kenya. He further indicates that the low quality of coffee in Brazil is attributed to the low soil quality, constantly changing climatic conditions and the country's altitude which are key determinants of the quality of coffee beans that are produced.

Ethiopia has been argued to have some of the best quality coffee in the world (World Bank, 2012). Dorothy (2013) also argues that the level of sweepings in marketing coffee from Ethiopia negatively influence the contract price. Although coffee from Columbia has higher quality in terms of taste and appearance, the grading of coffee from Ethiopia is more preferred in the world market (Beanposter, 2012)

Columbia has specialized in growing the Arabica coffee and is recognized worldwide for production of highest quality of coffee with a distinctive taste (Beanposter, 2012). In addition, the coffee produced in Columbia is of profound appearance with good brightness, body and flavour. Nevertheless, the types of cartels that are involved in marketing coffee have negative impact on the lead time for payment and the final contract price for the product. This lead to the low level of production with majority of the farmers preferring other types of cash crops that garner them relatively higher profits (Mafusire, Salami, Kamara & Lawson, 2010).

According to Brian (2010), the indicators of the performance of coffee industry are the contract price. Although Kalyango (2013) agrees with Brian (2010) he also argues that lead time for payments is an indicator of performance of coffee industry. While undertaking industry analysis at the macro-economic levels of the Asian Giants, Kalyango (2013) adds that the ratio of farm price to auction price is the going

1

concern in the coffee sector. As such, the farm price to auction price, lead time for payment and contract price have been identified in this study as the indicators of performance of the coffee industry.

In USA, Crude oil, coffee and gas are the three most traded commodities in international markets. No other agriculture commodity can compete with the trade volumes of crude oil and gas than coffee. Coffee is the queen of all agriculture commodities when it comes to the volume of international trade. Unlike tea, coffee is mostly consumed by developed nations such as the United States and European countries but produced by developing countries such as Brazil, Columbia, Indonesia and Vietnam. The coffee demand-supply web makes coffee truly an international commodity. Economic performance of both exporting and the U.S fuels coffee retail prices. International Coffee Agreement and NYBOT.coffee prices/spot prices are the two most important factors that impact retail prices of coffee in the United States.

Brazil is unquestionably the biggest coffee producing country in the world. With a seemingly endless expense available for its production, coffee plantations in Brazil often cover immense areas of land, need hundreds of people to manage and operate them, and produce huge quantities of coffee. A 'Brazilian' coffee is a 'mild' and the two terms are often used interchangeably. Both arabica and robusta are grown, though in different coffee growing regions. The ambient climate, soil quality and altitude largely determine which variety will grow best in which region. A fine cup of Brazilian is a clear, sweet, medium-bodied, low-acid coffee.

Indonesia, one of the world's largest countries, is composed of thousands of islands. Several of the larger islands -- Sumatra, Java and Sulawesi (or Celebes as it was called) -- are known throughout the world for the fine, quality coffees which grow there. The coffee plant was introduced to Indonesia by Dutch colonists in the 17th century and soon led the world's production. Today, small coffee farms of 1-2 acres predominate and most of it is dry processed. Indonesian coffees are noted for a pronounced rich, full body and mild acidity. Indonesia is also known for its fine aged coffees. Traditionally, these were coffees held over a period of time by farmers who wanted to sell them at higher prices. Warehousing, it was found, gently aged the coffee in Indonesia's warm, damp climate and resulted in an coffee prized for even deeper body and less acidity. It is a process which cannot been matched by technology.

In Tanzania coffee accounts for about 20% of Tanzania's foreign exchange earnings and has been the mainstay of the country's agriculture-based economy since its introduction as a cash crop around 100 years ago. More than 450,000 farm families

(95%) and 110 estates (5%) derive their livelihoods from growing coffee with an estimated 2,000,000 additional people employed being directly or indirectly in the industry. Coffee production is concentrated in five main geographic areas of Tanzania, in the north (Kilimanjaro, Arusha & Tarime), in the west (Kigoma & Kagera) and south (Mbeya, Iringa and Ruvuma). However, despite this situation, Tanzania is very well suited to coffee production (and in particular the production of less price-sensitive Arabica coffee) because of its expansive volcanic highland areas and the Great Lakes basin which provide ideal conditions for growing coffee. There is great potential for developing the Industry.

Ethiopia is the origin of coffee Arabica, and it grows wide variety of exemplary coffee, highly differentiated, most of which are shade-grown by small farmers without chemical inputs (Dempsey 2006). Ethiopia is the largest producer of coffee and ranks fifth in the world and first in Africa by annual coffee production. For the past three to four decades, coffee has been and remains the leading cash crop and major export commodity of the country. Coffee accounts on average for about 10% of total agricultural production, 5% of Gross Domestic Product, and constitutes about 41% of total export earnings of the country (Worako 2008). Factors such as education, proportion of land allocated to coffee, proportion of off farm income to total income, coop performance, satisfaction on coop performance, and second payment affect affected market outlet choice in Ethiopia. While age of the household head, proportion of off farm income, and access to training has positively influenced non member coffee grower's buyer selection decision. Finally the study confirmed the continued viability of coffee marketing cooperatives as suppliers of coffee to coffee buyers in the study area.

Kenyan coffee is well-known and well-liked, both in the United States and Europe. Kenyan beans produce a singular cup with a sharp, fruity acidity, combined with full body and rich fragrance. Coffee is grown on the foothills of Mount Kenya, often by small farmers. Kenyan producers place an emphasis on quality and as a result, processing and drying procedures are carefully controlled and monitored. Kenya has its own unique grading system. Kenyan AA is the largest bean in a 10-size grading system and AA+ means that it was estate grown.

Problem Statement

For a long period of time, coffee was a major agricultural export for Kenya accounting for about 40% of the total income earned on exports. This has dramatically changed since 1988 with coffee currently accounting for 6% of the total agricultural exports (Monroy, Mulinge, & Witwer, 2013). Coffee farming in Kenya has lately been influenced by decreased contract price despite the high marketing and processing costs that are borne by the farmer. Production has also been affected with the farmers incurring escalated costs in the recent past owing to the increased cost of farm inputs, currency devaluation, inefficient market inputs, inflation and poor infrastructures. In reality, majority of the farmers make losses and are always in debt owing to the long lead time for payment which has contributed to coffee neglect and the coffee growers living in abject poverty (Nyoro & Karanja, 2002).

The performance of the coffee industry is Kenya has been greatly influenced by the loose controls that were introduced in the sector in 2001 (Gitu, 2012). It is at this point that the Government of Kenya stopped their engagement in the management of cooperatives, they allowed farmers to decide whether to use the marketing agents, millers or pulping factories, they ended their financial assistance to the Coffee Research foundation and coffee cooperatives, there was privatization of the coffee auctions with some coffee evading the auctioneers and by being sold directly to the exporters, the role of Coffee board of Kenya as the regulator was limited and also tremendously increased the marketing licenses allowed to twenty-five.

According to Mude (2006), the government maintained a zero graft in the coffee cooperatives through the election of District Cooperative Officers (DCOs). The DCOs protected the small scale farmer most of whom have low skills, low level of education as well as have little political affluence by attending the general meetings, ensuring there was free and fair election and making their mark during issuance of loans and disbursement of dividends to members. With the introduction of liberalized policies, the DCOs designation changed to being the advisors to the cooperative societies and reporting the progress of cooperatives in their Districts. Gitu (2012) asserts that the loss of affluence by the DCOs is detrimental to the coffee cooperatives as it has led to a drastic rise in corruption with the rich taking the lead. Therefore, lack of accountability by the corrupt managers and committee members has eventually led to inflated operating costs and reduced contract price.

According to Nyoro & Karanja (2002), the current policy objective is to increase production of coffee, value addition, availing affordable credit to the coffee growers as well as increasing market accessibility. Nevertheless, the Coffee board of Kenya, which is bestowed with the regulatory responsibilities, has failed in formulation of prudent policies that promote Kenyan coffee globally. Okoth (2013) asserts that the policies and rules formulated by the board are prohibitive, illegal, pro-cartels, anti-coffee growers and inconsistent with the constitution and Agriculture, Fisheries and Food Authority act, 2013.

Despite Kenya having worldwide reputation on its production of high quality coffee with outstanding appearance and taste, the performance of coffee industry is diminishing drastically as time progresses. Therefore, this study will seek to determine the factors that influence the performance of coffee industry in Kenya.

Objectives of the Study

The broad objective of the study is to assess the factors that affect the performance of coffee industry in Kenya.

The specific objectives of the study are:

i. To determine the extent to which quality of coffee impacts on performance of coffee industry
ii. To establish how government policy influence performance of coffee industry
iii. To investigate the extent to which the growers capacity affects performance of coffee industry
iv. To determine the extent to which marketing processes influence the performance of coffee industry.

Research questions

i. To what extent does the quality of coffee affect performance of the coffee industry in Mathira constituency?
ii. How does government policy influence performance of coffee industry in Mathira constituency?
iii. To what extent does the grower's capacity affect performance of the coffee industry in Mathira constituency?
iv. In what ways does marketing process influence the performance of coffee industry in Mathira constituency?

Significance of the Study

This study was projected to provide essential information to the variety of stakeholders involved in the coffee industry. These stakeholders include but not limited to regulatory bodies, policy makers, academia, coffee cooperative societies and coffee farmers. The study exposed the different economic and market factors that affect coffee industry right from production to the sale of the product either through the auctioneers or direct export. The regulatory bodies and policy makers should be enlightened on their faults in creating unfavourable avenues for the growth of the coffee industries. To the cooperative societies and coffee farmers, the study drew attention on the shortcomings of the coffee industry thus being a good source of information for decision making.

Scope of Study

Mathira constituency is located in Nyeri County in Nyeri North district. According to the census report carried out by KNBS (2009) the area has a population of 148,847 people occupying an area of 296.60 Sq. Km. The area is located in Nyeri county which according to Wangechi (2014) has an altitude of 1220 to 2300m with an average rainfall of 953mm and is bestowed with rich red volcanic soils. These conditions are favourable for production of high quality coffee. The study was carried out between January and March 2015.

Limitations of the Study

The limitations of the study are lack of adequate past research and data. The other limitation was hostile cartels that interfered with the research. To overcome the limitations the study had to carry out a pilot in order to anticipate and overcome expected limitations. The limitation included suspicion from the side of the respondents and this was overcome by providing an introductory letter from M.U.A and assuring the respondents of the confidentiality for information they provided.

Another limitation was language barrier. To overcome this limitation the researcher read and interpreted the questions to all the respondents who could not read and understand English language. Large study area to be covered also posed challenges to this study. The researcher had to invest extra time to ensure that all the respondents were reached.

Summary

In this chapter, background information about the research topic was discussed. The study analysed the performance of coffee industry in different regions. This was aimed painting a clear picture of how coffee sector was performing in developed and in developing countries for comparison purposes. This chapter also highlighted the statement of the problem that necessitated carrying out of this research. In addition, this chapter also contain objectives of the study, research question, scope of the study and limitations the researcher faced and how they were overcame.

CHAPTER TWO
LITERATURE REVIEW

Introduction

This section presents the theoretical review, empirical review and conceptual framework of the study. The review will provide the previous contributions of different authors to the problem with their findings providing a basis for identifying the research gaps which are the entry point for this survey.

Theoretical Review

This research is anchored in the public interest theory of regulation, total quality management theory and Theory of Performance were examined. The three theories provide a basis for people's motivation to performance of duty.

Public Interest Theories of Regulation

The first group of regulation theories account for regulation from the point of view of aiming for public interest. This public interest can be further described as the best possible allocation of scarce resources for individual and collective goods. In western economies, the allocation of scarce resources is to a significant extent coordinated by the market mechanism. In theory, it can even be demonstrated that, under certain circumstances, the allocation of resources by means of the market mechanism is optimal (Arrow, 1985). Because these conditions are frequently not adhered to in practice, the allocation of resources is not optimal and a demand for methods for improving the allocation arises (Bator, 1958). One of the methods of achieving efficiency in the allocation of resources is government regulation (Arrow, 1970; Shubik, 1970). According to public interest theory, government regulation is the instrument for overcoming the disadvantages of imperfect competition, unbalanced market operation, missing markets and undesirable market results.

In the first place, regulation can improve the allocation by facilitating, maintaining, or imitating market operation. The exchange of goods and production factors in markets assumes the definition, allocation and assertion of individual property rights and freedom to contract (Pejovich, 1979). The guarantee of property rights and any necessary enforcement of contract compliance can be more efficiently organized collectively than individually Furthermore, the costs of market transactions are reduced by property and contract law.

The freedom to contract can, however, also be used to achieve cooperation between parties opposed to market operation. Agreements between producers give rise to

7

prices deviating from the marginal costs and an inefficient quantity of goods is put on the market. Antimonopoly legislation is aimed at maintaining the market operation through monitoring the creation of positions of economic power and by prohibiting competition limiting agreements or punishing the misuse thereof.

This theory is deemed relevant since it informs the government policy which is one of the variables in this study. Government may regulate the performance of coffee industry either by providing tax incentives or subsidies to the growers.

Total Quality Management Theories

Scudder (2013) argues that Total Quality Management (TQM) is a quality improvement body of methodologies that are customer-based and service oriented. TQM was first developed in Japan, and then spread in popularity. However, while TQM may refer to a set of customer based practices that intend to improve quality and promote process improvement, there are several different theories at work guiding TQM practices. A popular TQM theory is Deming's theory of Total Quality Management .The theory rests upon fourteen points of management he identified, the system of profound knowledge, and the Shewart Cycle (Plan-Do-Check-Act). He is known for his ratio - Quality is equal to the result of work efforts over the total costs. If a company is to focus on costs, the problem is that costs rise while quality deteriorates. Deming's system of profound knowledge consists of the following four points: System Appreciation which explains an understanding of the way that the company's processes and systems work, Variation Knowledge which explains an understanding of the variation occurring and the causes of the variation, Knowledge Theory which explains the understanding of what can be known and Psychology Knowledge which examine the understanding of human nature. This theory is deemed relevant since it informs the quality of coffee variable

Theory of Performance

According to Lawler (2000) the theory of performance revolves around six components to explain performance and performance improvements. These components are skill levels, knowledge levels, context, identity level, fixed factors and personal factors. Skills level determines the actions executed by an individual or organization so as to obtain a favourable end product. Knowledge levels possessed by individuals provide them with concepts, facts, information and principles that provide guidance in one's life and experiences. Context in which one lives determines their decision making based on the surrounding exposures. Identity level is acquired as an individual or an organization matures in a discipline and they grow by picking up from the community and at the same time develop their own

8

uniqueness. Fixed factors are usually unique characteristics of an individual that cannot be changed whereas the personal factors are developed in accordance with the situations that an individual is exposed to. All these factors are essential in determination of performance of an individual, organization or an industry.

Elger (2014) in his rationale for performance theory indicates that human beings are able to accomplish extraordinary things in the universe. For example, humans can go to the moon and carry out other activities not because of their ease but because they are hard since the objective will be to measure and organize the individual's skills and energies. He refers to performance as a journey that is classified into levels in which the higher the level the higher the quality and level of effectiveness. The theory recognizes the characteristics of higher performance level to be capability and capacity of the activity, knowledge and skills level, cost effectiveness, quality of the product or the resultant factor and finally motivation and identity (Tomlinson et al, 2002).

The theory of performance is also based on several axioms for effectiveness in improvement of performance. These include immersion, performer's mind-set and engagement in reflective practice (Sonnentag & Frese, 2001). Immersion into one's environment enables one to develop physically, intellectually and socially hence improving one's social relations, emotions, active learning, and knowledge alignment.

To ensure high level of performance the performer's mind-set is a very essential factor as it engages positive emotions towards the activity and enables the performer to consider failure as a stepping stone to achieving high level of performance. In this regard the farmer's mind-set is essential in decision making on whether to invest in coffee farming or divert to other avenues of production for better profits (Bransford, Brown & Cocking, 2000). Reflective practice creates a platform for one to observe the current performance of an industry, examine the accomplishments, carry out an analysis of strengths, weaknesses, improvements and develop identity thus working for the improvement of the entity.

Empirical Literature Review

Quality of Coffee and Performance

Kirumba & Pinard (2010) conducted a study on the factors that determine the compliance of farmers with the recommended standards for coffee eco-certification .The study used the binary logistic regression model to show that socio-economic, institutional factors and farm characteristics are of essence in farmer's certification.

The findings of the study showed that the farmer's perception on the benefits of coffee, annual production of coffee, spraying of the coffee crop and having coffee as key source of income are the determining factors for compliance to certification. The study further pointed out the financial status of the farmer as a growing concern for certification since the certifiers concentrate on the progressive farmers and leave out the weak farmers the study concentrates on the growers capacity but less is said on the ratio of farm price to auction price, government policies, contract price as well as lead time for payment which play an imperative role in demand for certification.

Mwangome (2011) indicated that liberalization of coffee marketing rules led to increase in price per kilogram between 2004 and 2008, there was increased income by the farmers with the percentage pay out increasing from 65% to 83%, and a substantial reduction of coffee output. The reduced production was associated with changes in weather patterns as well settlement in the areas that were previously coffee farms due to increase in population in the area. The study further identified that the coffee quality in the area is still high owing to introduction of improved coffee varieties and increased price incentives fetched from the high quality coffee. The study identified the need to reduce marketing agents, reduce taxation on coffee, infrastructural development, introducing strict regulation as well as expanding the international markets for coffee. Despite the indicated increase in coffee prices the study did not consider the diminished growers capacity as well as put into consideration the demotivation to the farmers as a result of lead time for payment and ratio of farm price to auction price.

The constraints faced by small scale coffee producers have contributed in the production of low quantity of coffee with relatively low quality. According to USAID (2010), these constraints include low capital with limited access to credit, lack of adequate knowledge on farm management, failure to adopt varieties that are resistant to diseases, lack of quality premiums and poor economies of scale in the cooperative societies. The value chain analysis study further highlights the use of obsolete equipment which was installed during the colonial times as a major problem that affects wet processing of coffee in the country hence exporting most of the locally produced coffee. Poor management of cooperatives is also detrimental to the coffee industry. Despite the study identifying the most critical factors leading to the decline of coffee production the government policies and poor payment of the coffee growers despite the high cost of Kenyan coffee in the market have not been adequately addressed.

Government Policy and Performance

Gathura (2013) conducted a study on the factors that influence production of coffee by small-scale farmers in Kenya. The establishments under study were small-scale coffee farms in Githunguri District. It was to determine whether marketing factors, finances, government policies and physical and human resources affect coffee production in Githunguri District. Primary sources included use of questionnaires, observation and interviews. Secondary sources included desk research, library research on journals, text books and factory publications. The target population was over 700,000 small-scale coffee producers in Kenya out of which the accessible population of 10,000 producers drawn from Githunguri District in Kiambu County was selected which a sample size of 120 respondents was sampled specifically, the study investigated the impact of marketing factors, financial constraints, government policies and human and physical resources on coffee production. The study utilized the descriptive statistics to provide the evidence that financial status, the emerging marketing trends in the coffee industry, physical and human resource factors as well as government policies are the key causes of the decline in the coffee industry. Nevertheless, the study did not factor in the quality of coffee, growers capacity with regard to knowledge levels and level of technology as essential factors that affect the coffee production in Kenya.

Okibo (2013) conducted a study on effects of coffee liberalization. The study indicates the failure by the government in production of coffee as a major foreign currency earner. The objectives of the study were to identify the effects of deregulating co-operative societies, effects of switching the management of co-operative societies to farmers' committees and impact of licensing many marketing agents and coffee millers. The research findings provided the evidence that liberalization led to a decrease in coffee production. This was associated with the poor management of the co-operative societies, reduced utilization of modernized farm inputs, poor farming techniques, reduced earnings by the farmers and lack of confidence with the new management. The study mainly focused on liberalization policies but there was little attention on the low level of education by the small-scale farmers which contributed majorly in lack of counter attack strategy to the policies introduced by the government in early 1990s.

Growers Capacity and Performance

Mugweru, (2011), conducted a study on finding out the determinants of coffee production in the Kenyan economy he used a Nerlovian model to estimate supply response of coffee to these determinants and found out that there was appositive

11

relationship between price and coffee 7 outputs, output and rainfall, output and hectare planted and coffee output and price of input. The recommendation was that the government had to intervene by addressing the credit constraints and other factors contributing to a negative change of the above mentioned determinants so the study give the current study a better understanding of the possible factor which might be a current problem hence contributing to the decline in coffee.

Wangari (2010) conducted a study on factor that contributes to the declining trend of coffee production in Kenya: the case in Nyeri County. The assessment was done using descriptive statistics where OLS model was used to analyze the factors which could be affecting coffee production. The study used primary data collected from the interviewed sample of 30 farmers. The result of the study found out that produce price, growers capacity, distance to market and visit by extension officers to be the major factors that had significant impact on coffee production. The study offered some recommendation on how the above mentioned factors could be addressed to enhance a reverse in the coffee production trend.

Karanja (1998) in his study mentioned that in an effort to enhance coffee production, major changes had been introduced into the way. Coffee planters were licensed. In 1996, the minimum acreage required for a farmer to be licensed as a coffee planter was reduced from 10 to 5 acres. That change had resulted in a doubling of the number of small estates (below 20 acres) from 630 in 1994 to over1500 in 2000. Thus, the co-operatives continued to lose a sizeable number of their well to-do members as that became licensed as planters. That had further lowered the capacity utilization of those coffee-pulping factories owned by co-operatives while creating an increasingly, important group of medium-sized coffee producers. The small estates like other estate farmers were able to process their coffee separately and therefore had more' incentives to improve on their coffee quality unlike smallholder farmers who had to pool their cherry at the co-operative factories.

Marketing Processes and Performance

Mwongombe (2011) conducted a study on Impact of the liberalization of coffee marketing rules on the performance of coffee industry in Kenya: a survey of coffee farmers' co-operative societies in Mathira Division, Nyeri District. The target population was the managers and management committee officials of the coffee farmers' cooperative societies in the Division. A sample size of 36 managers out of a population of 60 and 27 management officials out of a population of 81 was targeted. From the sample size of 63 out of a population of 141, 60 respondents were interviewed. Questionnaires were used as the main data collection instruments for both groups of the respondents. The finding reveals that since the coming into effect of the new liberal marketing rules, coffee is fetching a higher price per kilogram than before. The price changed from, Ksh19 in 2004 to Ksh 34 in 2008.Coffee farmers income also increased from a percentage payout of 65.6% in 2004 to 83%'s in the year 2005. Coffee output though the average for the two time periods reflects an increase, but a substantial reduction in production for2008 from the 2007 level. This was attributed to change in weather patterns and settlement on previously coffee farms due to population pressures. However the quality of coffee is generally higher due to introduction of new or improved varieties and high price incentives on high quality coffee.

Theuri (2012) conducted a study which aimed at investigating the factors that influence revitalization of coffee programmes with the case study of Mukurweini district. He sought to investigate on accessibility of coffee markets, management and gender discrimination coexisting in the coffee co-operative societies. Descriptive statistics were used and they indicated that men dominate with regard to accessibility to credit, coffee crop ownership and control of income from coffee. The study further showed that proper marketing and good leadership are essential factors of coffee revitalization.

Karanja (2002) argued that the greatest threat to the social sustainability of coffee production results from the economic conditions facing coffee producers. They added that Coffee farmers typically depend upon coffee as their primary source of hard currency. As a result, declining and volatile coffee prices had a direct negative impact on access to education, housing, food, medical services and other basic necessities. David (2001) said that producer organizations can provide an important avenue for democratic, equitable representation and infrastructure development, the relative isolation of many small coffee farmers often places prohibitively high transaction costs on effective participation in such organizations. On the other hand, hired labor serving coffee plantations and estates typically represents the poorest segment of the population serving the supply chain. Although workers are not directly exposed to the vagaries of the market, evidence suggests that the performance of the market is transmitted to workers through poor general working conditions among such plantations have also been reported to be below national requirements and there is increased child labor reported on coffee plantations in some countries

Critical Review

A study identified the key causes of a decline in coffee sector to be the financial status of individuals, marketing trends, government policies and human and physical factors. Liberalization was also addressed and the government is to blame for not putting the necessary measures to protect the small scale farmers from poor management by the well-off individuals in the sector. Accessibility of the coffee markets and gender discrimination has also been previously studied. The issue of certification of coffee farmers has been given attention and the various hitches to the flourishing of the coffee sector identified as the causative factors for lack of commitment in certification by the farmers.

It is clear from the reviews of this study that the coffee industry is diminishing drastically with only a few individuals accounting for the benefits at the expense of the small-scale farmers who are the majority. This study therefore builds on, but the work differs from the earlier studies in that it gives an in-depth look into the quality of product and growers capacity. Moreover, there is no published evidence on the factors affecting the performance of coffee production in Mathira Constituency. This therefore makes the study more scope based and the results obtained can be used for comparison with other coffee growing areas for generalization purposes.

Conceptual Framework

Figure 2.1shows the relationship between the dependent and independent variables to be tested in the study. The dependent variable in this study will be performance of coffee industry. The indicators of performance of coffee industry that will be studied herein are ratio of farm price to auction price, lead time for payment and contact price. The independent variables to be included in the study are quality of coffee, grower's capacity, government policies and marketing processes.

Quality of Coffee

Quality of coffee is an imperative in the determination of the performance of coffee industry. Different countries yield different quality of coffee due to their differing climatic conditions, varied soil acidity and employment of different processing mechanisms. This therefore triggers the need to determine the impact of the grade of coffee, the taste, appearance and level of acidity in the performance of the coffee industry.

Grower's Capacity

The hitches faced by coffee producers have contributed in the production of low quantity of coffee with relatively low quality. The trainings offered by the extension workers are inadequate with the effect on the knowledge levels of coffee farmers. This study will therefore examine the extent to which the type of skills possessed by the coffee farmers, their level of education and lack of modern technologies affect the performance of the coffee industry.

Government Policy

The government of Kenya contributes immensely in the current performance of the coffee industry. It is involved in formulation of policies that govern the agricultural industry and the rules set forth may affect the performance either negatively or positively. In 1990s, the government of Kenya liberalized the coffee industry with the aim of increasing production and hence promoting foreign exchange earnings as well as increased income by farmers. Nevertheless, the production has continuously reduced and the coffee sector continues to experience depression. Therefore, this study seeks to determine the influence of the different type of formulated policies, their flexibility and enforceability in the performance of the coffee sector

Marketing Process

The marketing processes employed in the coffee sector in Kenya largely contribute in the determination of ratio of farm price to auction price, lead time for payment and contract price of the product. The channels used by the farmer to market their produce determine the final price. Farmers can either sell directly to the market or indirectly through the cartels. The final price is determined depending on the samples, level of sweepings and the type of cartels. Therefore, the study will determine the extent to which these marketing factors influence the performance of the coffee industry

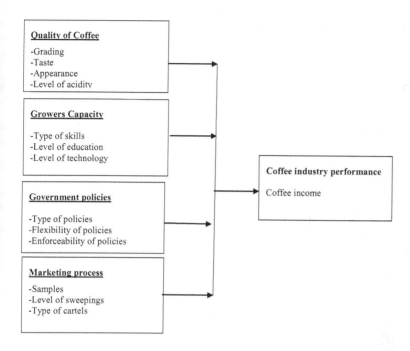

Figure 2.1   Conceptual framework

Summary of Literature Review

The literature review consisted of the theoretical review, empirical review and the conceptual framework. The theories studied herein are the public interest theory of regulation, total quality management theory and Theory of Performance. Public interest theory of regulation is based on his realization that the government may regulate the performance of coffee industry. TQT indicates that individuals strive to ensure that the quality of coffee is improved so as to earn better returns. The theory of performance indicate that the skill levels, knowledge levels, context in which one lives, identity level, fixed factors and personal factors of an individual are imperative for improved performance.

The findings of different authors in the empirical review provide a vivid picture of the challenges encountered in the coffee sector in Kenya converting the once a major foreign income earner cash crop to an agricultural area where no farmer is willing to venture into. The challenges such as unaffordable credit facilities, inadequate knowledge, lack of quality premiums and poor economies of scale in the cooperative societies, low level of technology and use of obsolete equipment among others have been studied. The conceptual framework shows the relationship between the dependent and independent variables to be tested in the study. A lot has been studied on the marketing factors, financial constraints, government policies and human and physical resources on coffee production but the problems still persist. Therefore, there is need to collect contextualized data for furthering knowledge on the factors that affect the performance of the coffee industry in Kenya.

CHAPTER THREE
RESEARCH METHODOLOGY

Introduction

This section provides information on the techniques and methods that were used to obtain the required data for the study. It present the Research design, Area of study, Target population, Sampling techniques and sample size, Data collection techniques and instruments, Data collection procedure, Data analysis and Ethical issues.

Research Design

This refers to the strategy that is employed to generate the required answers to the problems under investigation. The mixed mode research approach was used in this study. Specifically, the descriptive research design and correlation research design were employed. Descriptive research design enhanced clear examination of the research topic and also facilitated data collection process by answering questions concerning the study as per the current status. On the other hand, correlational research design provided a platform for the determination of the strength of the relationship between two or more variables (Gravetter & Forzano, 2011).

Mugenda and Mugenda (2003) indicates that descriptive design reports on the subject of study as it really is and provides a platform for the researcher to describe a phenomenon in terms of values, attitude, opinion and characteristics. A descriptive survey entails the collection of information by administering a questionnaire to a sample from the entire population of study. This design was efficient for this study since it enabled the subject to be observed in an absolutely unchanged and natural environment hence eliminating the possibility of researcher bias (Shuttleworth, 2008).

According to Mitchell & Jolley, (2012) correlational studies enable the researcher to seek conditions, abilities and traits that are corresponding with each other. For this reason, the results obtained through correlation help in making future predictions about a variable based on what is known of another.

Target Population

Target population refers to objects, cases or individuals with some characteristics that can be observed to make sound conclusion (Mugenda and Mugenda, 2003). The study targeted the managers of coffee cooperative societies and coffee farmers in

Mathira constituency. The study used primary data collected from a representative sample of the entire population via questionnaires which was used to solicit information as per the objectives of this study. The target population in this study was 26, 000 coffee farmers inclusive of factory managers in Mathira constituency.

Sampling Techniques and the Sample

Simple random sampling technique was used in this study. According to Mugenda & Mugenda (2003) the sample size used in a study is dependent on the research design, the size of the population that is accessible, number of variables and the method of data analysis. For descriptive surveys that yield quantitative data the fisher's formula was used to calculate the most appropriate sample size. Fisher's formula was suitable for this study since the target population was more than 10,000. The most essential indicators when using this formula are confidence or risk level, precision level or the sampling error and degree of variability (Israel, 2014).

The level of precision refers to the range within which the true value in the population lies and in this case we considered it to be ±5%. The confidence level shows the extent to which the value of an attribute is equal to the value in the true population when the population is repeatedly sampled. In this case the confidence level to be used was 95%. Degree of variability showed the level of distribution of different attributes in the study population (Kasiulevicius, Sapoka & Filipaviciue, 2006). A more heterogeneous population requires a large sample size to obtain the most desired precision level whereas a homogeneous population requires a small sample size. This study used the maximum variability which was 0.5.

The formula used was:

$$n = \frac{Z^2 pq}{e^2}$$

Where:

n represents the expected sample size

Z represents the abscissa if a curve that is normal and cuts the area α at the tails that is 1 − α which is equal to the desired level of confidence level which is 95% in this case

P represents an estimated proportion of a population attribute

q Is obtained by calculating 1-p

e represents the desired precision level

Therefore a sample size of 385 was obtained as follows:

$$n= \frac{(1.96)^2 \ (0.5) \ (0.5)}{(0.05)^2}$$

=385 respondents

Data Collection Techniques and Instruments

Primary data was utilized in this study to enhance originality of the study. Primary data was of essence in this study as it allowed the researcher to address issues that are specific to their study. Mugenda and Mugenda (2003) asserts that primary data enables the researcher to have control on how information will be collected and give him freedom to decide on the sample size, location of the research and time.

Primary data was collected from respondents via questionnaires. The questionnaires were administered to the coffee cooperative society managers, who are the project representatives, and to the randomly selected members of the community by the researcher. The questionnaire comprised of the questions that intended to answer the questions formulated with reference to the objectives of the study and the research questions. A questionnaire technique enabled the researcher find out what the respondents do, think and feel about the performance of coffee industry. The questionnaire included both closed and open ended questions to enhance uniformity and collection of maximum data respectively.

Data Collection Procedure

Data collection was carried out by use of questionnaires. The researcher furnished the respondents with an introductory letter issued by the university to instill confidence into the respondents. The respondents were not required to give their personal details such as names to ensure that they give detailed, reliable and accurate information without prejudice. The questionnaires were not be interpreted due to the assumption that the target population was literate. The researcher issued the questionnaires to the respondents on one on one interaction and give guidance when need arose

20

Data Validity and Reliability

Piloting was carried out to assess the ability of research instruments in collecting viable and reliable data that corresponded to the objectives of the study. It took place prior to the actual research. According to Mugenda and Mugenda (2003) it is adequate to use 1% to 10% of the sample size for pilot study. The pilot study was considered to be a way of pre-testing the data collection instruments and techniques hence identifying any ambiguity in the research question for rectification before the actual research. Validity refers to the extent to which the research measures what it is purported to measure (Sagor, 2000).

According to Sagor (2000) reliability helps to check the accuracy and consistency of the research results to ensure generalizability of the results obtained to the population. This study used the test-retest method which involved administration of the research instruments twice to the same individuals after a certain time lapse (Cooper & Schindler, 2000). In this case, a time lapse of two weeks was used. To test reliability, the questionnaires were administered to 10 respondents. Who included 3 coffee cooperative society managers and 7 coffee farmers in another Constituency. The Cronbach's α Reliability Coefficients was further used to measure reliability of the research instruments. A Cronbach's α Reliability Coefficients of α > 0.7 was acceptable.

Data Analysis

Data analysis involves the reduction of accumulated data to a controllable size, developing summaries, looking for patterns, and applying statistical techniques (Cooper and Schindler, 2000). The study used the quantitative method of data analysis. Data analysis played an important role in conversion of raw data into a form that can be subjected to statistical interpretation and presentation. The collected data was edited, coded, keyed in and analysed using Statistical Package for Social Sciences (SPSS).

The research yielded quantitative and qualitative data. The quantitative data was analysed using both descriptive statistics and correlations. Descriptive statistics helped to get the measures of central tendency and measures of dispersion which included the mean and standard deviation. The Pearson product movement correlation coefficient (r) was used to determine the strength of the relationship between different variables by use of the correlation coefficient, r, with a confidence interval of 95%. This helped in showing the strength of the relationship whereby an r value of ± 0.1 - ± 0.29 shows a weak relationship, an r value of ± 0.3 - ± 0.59 show a moderate relationship whereas an r value of ± 0.6 - ± 1 shows a strong relationship.

A simple regression model will be used to test the significance of the influence of the independent variables on the dependent variable. The multiple regression model will be as laid below.

$$Y = \beta_0 + \beta_1 X_1 + \beta_2 X_2 + \beta_3 X_3 + \beta_4 X_4 + e$$

Where:
Y = coffee industry performance

X_1 = quality of coffee

X_2 = grower's capacity

X_3 = government Policy

X_4 = marketing process

e= error term

Ethical Issues

The researcher upheld ethical issues in the process of the study and gave respondents assurance that confidentiality was observed and data collected was to be used for research purposes only.

The researcher obtained an informed consent from every respondent and all the relevant authorities were consulted. The researcher sought permission to collect all the necessary data required.

CHAPTER FOUR

DATA ANALYSIS, RESULTS PRESENTATION AND DISCUSSION

Introduction

This chapter comprises of data analysis, findings and interpretation. Results are presented in tables and diagrams. The analyzed data was arranged under themes that reflect the research objectives.

Response Rate

The number of questionnaires that were administered was 414. A total of 394 questionnaires were properly filled and returned. This represented an overall successful response rate of 95.2% as shown on Table 4.1. According to Mugenda and Mugenda (2003) and also Kothari (2004) a response rate of 50% is adequate for a descriptive study. Babbie (2004) also asserted that return rates of 50% are acceptable to analyze and publish, 60% is good and 70% is very good.

Table 4.1: Response Rate

Response	Frequency	Percent
Returned	396	95.2%
Unreturned	20	4.8%
Total	**416**	**100%**

Demographic Characteristics

This section consists of information that describes basic characteristics such as age of respondents, level of education, size of land under coffee and years they have practiced agriculture. The gender of the respondents is also given.

Gender of the Respondents

The respondents were asked to indicate their gender. Majority of the respondents were male who were represented 55% of the sample while 45% were female. The figure below shows the results.

23

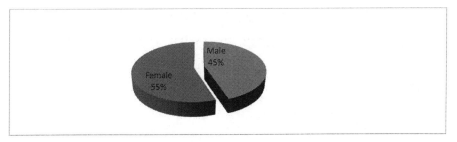

Figure 4.1: Gender of Respondents

Members of Cooperative Society

The respondents were asked to indicate whether they were members of a cooperative society or not. Result in figure 4.2 shows that 96% of the respondents were members of cooperative societies while 4% were not members of the cooperative society as shown in the figure below.

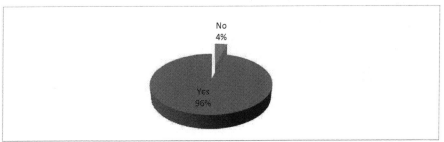

Figure 4.2: Members of Cooperative Society

Age

The respondents were asked to indicate their age bracket. Results in figure 4.3 shows that 60% of the respondents were over 50 years, 28% were between 41 to 50 years, 12% of the respondents were between 31 years to 40 years this indicate that those who were the majority were above 50 years.

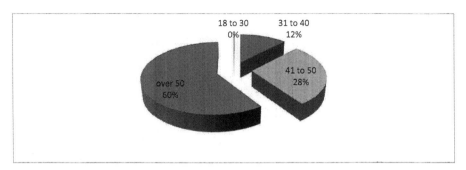

Figure 4.3: Age of the Respondents

Education Level of the Respondents

The respondents were asked to state their highest levels of education. Results in Figure 4.4 show that majority represented by 43% of the respondents had secondary qualifications, followed by primary level with 34% of the respondents while 6% of the respondents were certificate level and 6% of the respondents were diploma level while 7% and 1% of the respondents had bachelor's degree and masters respectively. This implies that majority of the respondents have a secondary education level as shown in the figure 4.4 below.

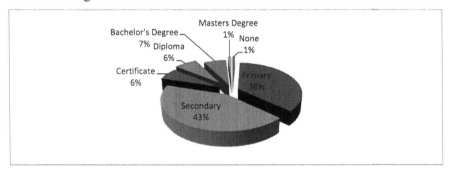

Figure 4.4: Level of Education

Monthly Income

The respondents were asked to indicate their monthly income generated from coffee farming. Results in figure 4.2.5 show that 35% of the respondents earned below ksh. 2200 while 33% of the respondents earned income of over ksh. 6001 while 32% represented respondents who earned between ksh. 2201 to 6000 this implies that majority of the respondents generated an income of below 2200 from coffee farming as shown in the figure below.

25

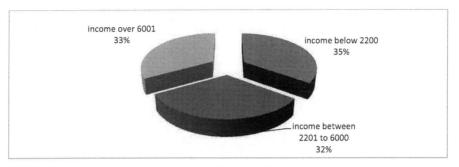

Figure 4.5: Income Generated from Coffee Farming

Income Come From Other Activities

The respondents were also asked to indicate the income they generated from other activities other than coffee farming. Results in figure 4.2.6 show that majority (74%) of the respondents were earning less than 10000 while 33% of the respondents earned income between 10001 and 30000 while 11% represented the respondents who earned over 30000 from other activities besides coffee farming.

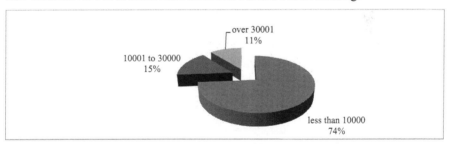

Figure 4.6: Income Generated from Other Activities

Land under Coffee

The respondents were asked to indicate the size of land under coffee. Results in figure 4.2.7 show that majority of the respondents represented by 93% had less than 4 acres under coffee while 1% of the respondents had between 4.1 and 10 acres of their land under coffee and finally 6% of the respondents had over 10 acres land under coffee. The study findings indicate that majority of the respondents were definitely not large scale coffee farmers as shown by the percentage of land under coffee. This can also be attributed to land fragmentation due to increase in population.

26

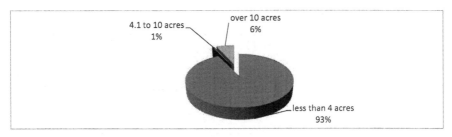

Figure 4.7:   Land under Coffee

Descriptive Statistics

This section presents the descriptive results on quality of coffee, grower's capacity, government policy, marketing processes and performance of coffee industry within the study area.

Quality of Coffee

The study sought to establish the effect of quality of coffee produced to general performance of coffee industry in Kenya. The responses were rated on a likert scale and the results presented in Table 4.2 below. Majority of the respondents represented by 28% disagreed that quality of coffee is affected by weather changes which lead to low performance of coffee industry in Kenya. As to whether poor soils affect the quality of coffee, 56% of the respondents were neutral. This suggests that majority of the respondents had no idea as to whether quality of coffee is affected by poor soil and whether this can affect the performance of coffee industry in Kenya. The respondents were also asked whether over fermentation of coffee during the peak season affected the taste and flavour of coffee leading to low performance. Majority of the respondents represented by 42% agreed with this statement. Majority of the respondents (37%) were also in agreement that poor branding of local coffee as of low quality led to low performance of coffee industry in Kenya. Finally as to whether reliance on sun drying led to lowers coffee quality hence affecting the selling price of coffee majority of the respondents (44.20%) disagreed does not necessarily lead to low performance of coffee industry. These results imply that quality of coffee produce locally had a relationship with the performance of coffee industry in Kenya. On a five point scale, the average mean of the responses was 4.016 which means that majority of the respondents agreed to the statements in the questionnaire; however the answers were varied as shown by a standard deviation of 1.51

27

Table 4.2: Quality of Coffee

Statement	Strongly Disagree	Disagree	Neutral	Agree	Strongly Agree	mean	Std.Dev
the grade of coffee is affected by the changes in weather which leads to low performance of coffee industry	0.50%	28.00%	23.20%	26.00%	22.20%	3.41	1.132
overutilization of soil without further improvement leads to lower taste of coffee and this leads to low performance	0.30%	4.00%	56.30%	29.50%	9.80%	3.95	0.736
over-fermentation of coffee during peak season affects the final taste and flavour of coffee and this leads to low performance	0.00%	10.40%	21.00%	42.50%	26.10%	4.84	0.929
lack of resources to brand local coffee lowers the selling price due to the poor quality and thus leads to low performance	5.60%	17.70%	21.50%	37.60%	17.70%	4.04	1.136
reliance on sun drying leads to a poor quality of coffee thus fetching lower prices hence low performance	12.40%	44.20%	27.50%	9.10%	6.80%	2.54	1.044
Average						4.016	0.9954

Grower's Capacity

The second objective of the study was to establish the effect of grower's capacity on coffe industry performance in Kenya. The results presented in Table 4.3 below show that 66.10 % of the respondents agreed that majority of coffee farmers have little information on coffee farming hence leading a low performance of the sector in Kenya. Majority (47%) of the respondents also agreed that pesticides and other coffee disease control chemicals are unaffordable which contributes to low performance of coffee industry in Kenya. Majority of the respondents represented by 61.90% attributed low performance to high fertilizer prices making fertilizers out of reach of many coffee farmers. As to whether small land size led to low production of coffee which encouraged shift to other food crops and thus leading to low performance of coffee industry majority (48.00%) of the respondents agreed. Majority of the respondents represented by 50.90% also agreed that lack of enough funds prevented them from venturing into large scale coffee farming and this also had a negative impact on the coffee industry in Kenya. Using a five point scale likert, the overall mean of the responses was 4.04 which indicates that majority of the respondents agreed to the statement in the questionnaire. Additionally, the standard deviation of 0.753 indicates that the responses were varied. The results herein imply that grower's capacity influences the performance of coffee industry in Kenya.

Table 4.3: Grower's Capacity

Statement	Strongly Disagree	Disagree	Neutral	Agree	Strongly Agree	mean	Std.Dev
majority of the coffee farmers have little information/training on coffee farming thus leading to low performance	0.80%	3.50%	15.20%	66.10%	14.40%	3.9	0.705
the pesticides used for coffee diseases and pest control are unaffordable to most farmers and thus leading to low performance	0.00%	3.30%	13.40%	47.00%	36.40%	4.16	0.777
fertilizer has become unaffordable owing to the high price vis a vis income gained from coffee and thus leading to low performance	0.00%	0.50%	7.80%	29.80%	61.90%	4.53	0.661
small land size leads to low production of coffee and encourage shift to food crops and thus leading to low performance of coffee industry	0.00%	14.60%	25.00%	48.00%	12.40%	3.58	0.886
financial constrains deter the small scale farmers from venturing into modern farming methods and thus leading to low performance	0.30%	1.30%	19.20%	50.80%	28.50%	4.06	0.74
Average						**4.046**	**0.7538**

Government Policy

The third objective of the study was to establish the effect of government policies on the performance of coffee industry in Kenya. The results are presented in table 4.4 show 52.50% of the respondents agreed that the withdrawal of farm inputs loans scheme affected the productivity of the farmers and thus leading to low performance of coffee. Further results show that high taxes imposed on farm inputs have

29

tremendous negative effects on coffee industry and thus leading to low performance as indicated by 26.30% of the respondents who agreed with the statement. Results also showed that 72.00%of the respondents agreed that CBK lacks accountability, transparency and order in its operations and thus lowering the performance of coffee industry. Further, results show that 73.90% of the respondents agreed that issuing of license to the major market players increases the sale of coffee cherries in the black market ("cherry hawking") and thus leading to low performance of coffee industry. Further, 78.80% of the respondents agreed that corruption and impunity in cooperatives is attributable to ignorance by the government and this leads to low performance of coffee industry. These results imply that the coffee industry in Kenya faces challenges posed by existing in policies. The average likert scale of the responses is 4.298 which indicates that majority of the respondents agreed to the statements. The standard deviation was 0.6968 which indicates that the responses were varied

Table 4.4: Government Policy

Statement	Strongly Disagree	Disagree	Neutral	Agree	Strongly Agree	Mean	Std. Dev
The withdrawal of farm inputs loans scheme affects the productivity of the farmers and thus leading to low performance of coffee	0.30%	3.50%	12.90%	52.50%	30.80%	4.1	0.77
The high taxes imposed on farm inputs have tremendous negative effects on coffee industry and thus leading to low performance	0.00%	32.30%	25.00%	26.30%	16.40%	3.27	1.083
The CBK lacks accountability, transparency and order on its operations and thus lowering the performance of coffee industry	0.00%	0.80%	2.50%	24.70%	72.00%	4.68	0.561
Issuing of license to the major market players increases the sale of coffee cherries in the black market("cherry hawking")and thus leading to low performance of coffee industry	0.00%	0.50%	1.80%	23.80%	73.90%	4.71	0.521
Corruption and impunity in cooperatives is attributable to ignorance by the government and this leads to low performance of coffee industry	0.00%	0.00%	5.30%	15.90%	78.80%	4.73	0.549
Average						**4.298**	**0.6968**

Marketing Process

The forth objective of the study was to establish the effect of marketing process on the coffee industry performance in Kenya. Results in table 4.5 show that 67.90% of the respondents agreed and strongly agreed that increased production cost accompanied by constant price fluctuations on coffee led to the decline in small scale farming while 82.30 % of the respondents agreed and strongly agreed that delays and inefficiencies by the marketing agents leads to increase in lead time for payment to the farmers and thus leading to low performance of coffee industry. Majority (40%) of the respondents disagreed that long distance to the market has negatively affected the production of coffee crop. Further, 47.80% of the respondents also disagreed that

31

poor roads led to delay in harvesting of coffee during rainy season thus low performance of coffee industry while 43.50% of the respondents disagreed that marketing and branding of Kenya coffee in the international markets is poor and thus low performance of coffee industry. On an average likert scale the responses had an overall mean of 3.458 which indicated that the respondents were neural to the majority of the questions asked. The standard deviation of 0.993 indicates that the responses small variation.

Table 4.5: Marketing Process

Statement	Strongly Disagree	Disagree	Neutral	Agree	Strongly Agree	Mean	Std. Dev
The increased production cost accompanied by constant price fluctuations on coffee led to the decline in small scale farming	0.00%	3.30%	28.80%	49.20%	18.70%	3.83	0.761
Delays and inefficiencies by the marketing agents leads to increase in lead time for payment to the farmers and thus low performance of coffee industry	0.00%	0.50%	17.20%	17.70%	64.60%	4.46	0.79
Long distance to the market has negatively affected the production of coffee crop	1.00%	39.10%	24.50%	13.40%	22.00%	3.16	1.192
Poor roads leads to delay in harvesting of coffee during rainy season thus low performance of coffee industry	1.80%	46.00%	24.20%	14.60%	13.40%	2.92	1.099
The marketing and branding of Kenya coffee in the international markets is poor and thus low performance of coffee industry	5.60%	37.90%	28.50%	15.20%	12.90%	2.92	1.124
Average						**3.458**	**0.9932**

Coffee Industry Performance

The main objective of the study was to assess the effects of quality of coffee, grower's capacity, government policy and marketing process on performance of coffee industry in Kenya. The table below shows the responses on the above statements. Majority of the respondents represented by 62.7% agreed and strongly agreed that poor quality of coffee has led to low performance of coffee industry while 78.50% agreed and strongly agreed that lack of proper government policies regarding to regulation of coffee industry has lead to low performance. On grower's capacity majority of the respondents represented by 83.60% agreed and strongly agreed that limited grower's capacity in coffee industry has led to low performance. On marketing processes the respondents had a varied view majority having a neutral view. The table below shows the responses.

Table 4.6: Coffee Industry Performance

Statement	Strongly Disagree	Disagree	Neutral	Agree	Strongly Agree	Mean	Std. Dev
poor quality of coffee has led to low performance of coffee industry	0.00%	4.50%	32.80%	40.70%	22.00%	3.8	0.832
lack of proper government policies regarding to regulation of coffee industry has lead to low performance	0.00%	2.80%	18.70%	37.60%	40.90%	4.17	0.825
limited growers capacity in coffee industry has led to low performance	0.00%	0.80%	15.70%	29.80%	53.80%	4.37	0.77
Poor marketing processes has led to low performance of coffee industry	9.05%	34.40%	29.20%	25%	2.35%	3.54	0.997
Average						**4.113**	**0.809**

Inferential Statistics

Inferential analysis was conducted to generate correlation results, model of fitness, and analysis of the variance and regression coefficients.

Correlation Analysis

The Table 4.6 below presents the results of the correlation analysis. The results presented in the Table 4.7 shows that quality of coffee and performance of coffee industry are positively and significant related (r=0.291, p=0.042). The table further indicates that grower's capacity and coffee industry performance are positively and significant related (r=0.359, p=0.000). The results further shows that government policies are positively and significantly related to coffee industry performance (r=0.415, p=.000). Similarly, results showed that marketing processes were positively and significantly related to coffee industry performance (r=0.101, p=.044).

Table 4.6: Correlation Matrix

	statistics	Overall quality of coffee	Overall growers capacity	Overall government policy	Overall marketing process	Overall coffee industry performance
Overall quality of coffee	r-value	1				
	p-value					
	N	396				
Overall growers capacity	r-value	-0.018	1			
	p-value	0.719				
	N	396	396			
Overall government policy	r-value	-.327**	.216**	1		
	p-value	0	0			
	N	396	396	396		
Overall marketing process	r-value	-0.062	0.076	-.117*	1	
	p-value	0.22	0.131	0.02		
	N	396	396	396	396	
Overall coffee industry performance	r-value	0.291*	.359**	.415**	.101*	1
	p-value	0.042	0	0	0.044	
	N	396	396	396	396	396

Regression Analysis

The results presented in table 4.7 present the fitness of model used in regression to explain the study phenomena. Quality of coffee, grower's capacity, government policy and marketing processes were found to be satisfactory variables in explaining coffee industry performance. This is supported by coefficient of determination also known as the R square of 28.0%. This means that the above variables explain 28.0 % of the variations in the dependent variable which is performance of coffee industry in Kenya. This result further suggests that the model applied to link the relationship of the variables was satisfactory.

Table 4.7: Model Fitness

Indicator	Coefficient
R	0.530
R Square	0.28
Adjusted R Square	0.273
Std. Error of the Estimate	0.5927

In statistics significance testing the p-value indicates the level of relation of the independent variable to the dependent variable. If the significance number found is less than the critical value also known as the probability value (p) which is statistically set at 0.05, then the conclusion would be that the model is significant in explaining the relationship; else the model would be regarded as non-significant.

Table 4.8 provides the results on the analysis of the variance (ANOVA). The results indicate that the overall model was statistically significant. Further, the results imply that the independent variables are good predictors of coffee industry performance. This was supported by an F statistic of 38.095 and the reported p value (0.000) which was less than the conventional probability value of 0.05 significance level.

Table 4.8: Analysis of Variance

Indicator	Sum of Squares	df	Mean Square	F	Sig.
Regression	53.531	4	13.383	38.095	0.000
Residual	137.358	391	0.351		
Total	190.889	395			

Regression coefficients results in table 4.9 shows that there is a positive and significant relationship between quality of coffee, grower's capacity, government policy and marketing processes and dependent variable which is coffee industry performance as supported by beta coefficients of 0.155, 0.431, 0.693 and 0.162 respectively. These results show that an increase in the 0.155 units in quality of coffee will result in unit increase in performance of coffee industry in Kenya. The results also suggest that an increase in 0.431 units in grower's capacity will result in a unit increase in performance of coffee industry. Increase by 0.693 units in appropriate government policies will have a unit increase in coffee industry performance while an increase in 0.162 in marketing process will have a corresponding increase of a unit in performance of coffee sector in Kenya.

Table 4.9: Regression of Coefficients

Variable	B	Std. Error	t	Sig.
(Constant)	1.692	0.509	3.321	0.001
Overall quality of coffee	0.155	0.05	3.077	0.002
Overall grower's capacity	0.431	0.073	5.867	0
Overall government policy	0.693	0.078	8.916	0
Overall marketing processes	0.162	0.051	3.196	0.002

The multiple linear regression model is as shown below.

$$Y = \beta_0 + \beta_1 X_1 + \beta_2 X_2 + \beta_3 X_3 + \beta_4 X_4 + e$$

Where:

Y = coffee industry performance

X_1 = quality of coffee

X_2 = grower's capacity

X_3 = government Policy

X_4 = marketing process

e= error term

Thus, the optimal model for the study is;

Coffee industry performance = **1.692** + **0.155***(quality of coffee)* + **0.431***(grower's capacity)* +**0.693***(government Policy)* + **0.162***(marketing process)* + *e*

CHAPTER FIVE:
SUMMARY, CONCLUSIONS AND RECOMMENDATIONS

Introduction

This chapter addresses the summary of the findings, the conclusions and the recommendations. This is done in line with the objectives of the study.

Summary of Findings

This section provides a summary of the findings from the analysis. The summary is done in line with the objectives of the study.

Quality of Coffee and Coffee Industry Performance

The first objective of the study was to establish the effect of quality of coffee produced on coffee industry performance. The results reveal that quality of coffee has impacted the performance of coffee industry in Kenya. Majority of the respondents agreed that the quality of coffee produced in Kenya is has affected the general performance of coffee industry in Kenya. This finding is further supported by the result of regression analysis carried out which shows that the quality of coffee produced have a significantly positive relationship with the performance of coffee industry in Kenya. From the regression analysis the study obtained a beta coefficient of 0.155 which suggests a positive and significant relation between the two variables.

These results imply that to boost the performance of coffee industry in Kenya players in this industry should employ strategies that will increase the quality of coffee produced. These findings agree with those of Kirumba & Pinard (2010) and Mwangome (2011) who found out that performance of coffee sector depends on selling prices which are dictated by the quality of coffee.

Grower's Capacity and coffee industry performance

The second objective of the study was to identify the effects of grower's capacity on coffee industry performance in Kenya. Results showed that grower's capacity have significant effects on coffee industry performance in Kenya. The results show that majority of the respondents represented by 83.60% agreed and strongly agreed that limited grower's capacity in coffee industry has led to low performance of coffee industry in Kenya. In addition the results indicated that grower's capacity has a positive and significant relationship with coffee industry performance. Further the results indicated that an increase of *0.431* will result in a corresponding one unit increase in performance of coffee industry in Kenya. This study finding is in line with that of Wangari (2010) and Karanja (1998) who found out that there was significant positive relationship between grower's capacity and performance of coffee industry in Kenya. Therefore efforts to revitalise performance of coffee industry should also be directed towards capacitating the farmers which will increase coffee production hence boosting the industry at large.

Government Policy and Coffee Industry Performance

The third objective of the study was to establish the effect of government policy and coffee industry performance. The findings showed that majority of the respondents (78.50%) agreed and strongly agreed that lack of proper government policies regarding to regulation of coffee industry has lead to low performance. Further results found that Increase by 0.693 units in appropriate government policies will have a unit increase in coffee industry performance. These results imply that the government of Kenya should revisit the policies and regulations and adopt new policies that will rejuvenate the coffee industry performance. These findings agree with those of Gathura (2013) conducted a study on the factors that influence production of coffee by small-scale farmers in Kenya and found out that marketing trend in the coffee industry, physical and human resource factors as well as government policies are the key causes of the decline in the coffee industry. The findings also agree with those of Okibo (2013) who conducted a study on effects of coffee liberalization. The study findings indicated that the government has failed in production of coffee as a foreign currency earner.

Marketing Process and Performance of Coffee Industry

The study sought to establish the effect of marketing process on coffee industry performance. The result shows that the respondents were neutral about marketing processes effects on performance of coffee industry. The respondents were divided in opinion with some agreeing and others disagreeing on the effects of marketing process on coffee industry performance. The regression analysis showed that an increase in 0.162 in marketing process will have a corresponding increase of a unit in performance of coffee sector in Kenya. These findings are in agreement with those of Mwongombe (2011) who conducted a study on Impact of the liberalization of coffee marketing rules on the performance of coffee industry in Kenya. Mwongombe's study finding reveals that since the coming into effect of the new liberal marketing rules, coffee is fetching a higher price per kilogram than before. The price changed from, Ksh19 in 2004 to Ksh 34 in 2008.Coffee farmers income also increased from a percentage payout of 65.6% in 2004 to 83%'s in the year 2005. Coffee output though the average for the two time periods reflects an increase, but a substantial reduction in production for2008 from the 2007 level. The findings of this study are also in line with those Theuri (2012) who conducted a study which aimed at investigating the factors that influence revitalization of coffee programmes with the case study of Mukurweini district. The study findings showed that proper marketing and good leadership are essential factors of coffee revitalization.

Coffee Industry Performance

The main objective of this study was to assess the factors that affect the performance of coffee industry in Kenya. The factors under investigation included quality of coffee, grower's capacity, government policy and marketing process. The study findings showed that all the factors have a positive significant relationship with the performance of coffee industry in Kenya. The factor combined accounted for 28% of the performance of coffee industry.

Quality of coffee had a significantly positive relationship with the performance of coffee industry in Kenya. From the regression analysis the study obtained a beta coefficient of 0.155 which suggests a positive and significant relation between the two variables. Grower's capacity has a positive significant effect on coffee industry performance in Kenya. Government policy also had a positive significant effect on the performance of coffee industry in Kenya as well as marketing process.

These findings agree with most of the previous study conducted on the topic. For instance the study findings agree with those of Gathura (2013) who conducted a study on the factors that influence production of coffee by small-scale farmers in Kenya. The establishments under study were small-scale coffee farms in Githunguri District. The factors under study included marketing factors, finances, government policies and physical and human resources affect coffee production in Githunguri District. The study utilized the descriptive statistics to provide the evidence that financial status, the emerging marketing trends in the coffee industry, physical and human resource factors as well as government policies are the key causes of the decline in the coffee industry.

Conclusions

Based on the findings above the study concluded that coffee industry performance requires a great deal of investment rise the standards and maintain a vigorous industry.The study also concluded that the quality of coffee produced is among the key factors that must be addressed to keep the coffee industry alive. The grower's capacity is another limiting factor to expansion of coffee industry. The study therefore concludes that lack of funds, knowledge in coffee farming and necessary farm inputs prevents full exploitation of coffee industry in Kenya.

Secondly, the study concluded that government policies affect the performance of coffee industry in Kenya. Policies such the withdrawal of Farm Inputs Loans Scheme, high taxes imposed on farm inputs, CBK lacks accountability and transparency and Corruption and impunity in cooperatives have contributed to low performance of coffee industry. The study therefore asserts that there is a positive and significant relationship between government policies and performance of coffee industry in Kenya.

Thirdly, the results concluded that marketing process have an influence coffee industry performance. This was guided by the findings that revealed that 67.90% of the respondents agreed and strongly agreed that marketing process played a significant role in the performance of coffee industry. The regression analysis showed that an increase in 0.162 in marketing process will have a corresponding increase of a unit in performance of coffee sector in Kenya. The study also concludes that to obtain an efficient working coffee industry a lot should be done as far marketing is concerned. The study also concludes that there exist a positive relationship between marketing process and performance of coffee industry in Kenya.

Recommendations

The following recommendations based on the study findings are suggested to help boost performance of coffee industry in Kenya. Production of coffee from harvesting to processing should be done in the manner that will maintain the high quality of final coffee which will attract high prices hence revitalizing the coffee industry. CBK should also intervene to train farmers on how to maintain healthy crops that will leads to high quality produce.

The study also recommends that the farmers should fetch high income from the coffee farming. High income will act as incentive to farmers to expand their coffee production and also farmers will have enough funds necessary to purchase farm inputs leading to the growth of the coffee industry. From the study findings most of the farmers who participate in coffee farming also participate in other income generating activities hence diverting their attention from coffee farming. With good income generated from coffee farming such farmers can be encouraged to be full time coffee farmers which will boost the production of coffee in Kenya. This will translate to buoyant coffee industry.

The coffee industry players and the government need to harmonize the policies regulating coffee industry in order to achieve a robust industry. The policies must be formulated with the benefits to farmers in mind and this will act as incentives to farmers to commit them to coffee farming. Farm Inputs Loans should be re-introduces, taxes on farm input harmonized, and the government should ensure that CBK is corruption free to pump new energy into the coffee industry. In addition, CBK should be accountable in its transactions; exploitative middlemen should be rooted out of the industry to lay proper grounds for rejuvenation of coffee industry in Kenya.

Lastly all key players should come up with new strategies to market Kenyan coffee in international markets to enable locally coffee to compete in international markets that will offer good prices for locally produced coffee. Good marketing strategies will also eliminate middlemen who exploit the farmers.

Areas for Further Studies

The study sought to assess factors that that affect coffee industry in Kenya, quality of coffee, grower's capacity, government policy and marketing process were assessed. Further studies could consider different factors such climatic factor, increase in population effects on performance of coffee industry. This study used Mathira constituency in Kenya as a case study therefore a similar study can be conducted with regard to another region for comparison purposes.

41

REFERENCES

BeanPoster, (2012). The top 3 countries for picking coffee beans: From the roasterie's Q grader. Kansas: The Roasterie Air- Roasted Coffee.

Bransford, J. D., Brown, A. L., Cocking, R. R., eds. (2000). *How people learn.* Washington DC: National Academy Press.

Cooper, D.R., & Schindler, P.S. (2000). *Business Research Methods.* New York: Irwin/ McGraw-Hill

Dempsey, J. (2006). A Case Study of Institution Building & Value Chain Strengthening to Link Ethiopian Cooperative Coffee Producers to International Markets. *Addis Ababa: ACDI/Voca.*

Dorothy, Nakaweesi. (2013). *Uganda's monthly coffee shipments on steady rise.* Daily Monitor (Kampala). Retrieved 2013-01-28.

Elger, D. (2014). *Theory of performance.* Moscow: University of Idaho.

Gathura, M. (2013). Factors affecting Small-Scale Coffee Production in Githunguri District, Kenya. *International Journal of Academic Research in Business and Social Sciences,* 3(9), 132-148

Gitu, S. (2012).*A Need for Better Organizational Capacity in Kenya's Coffee Cooperatives: A Case Study of New Gatanga Coffee Cooperative Society, Kenya.* Ontario: The University of Guelph.

Gravetter, F., & Forzano, L. (2011). Research Methods for the Behavioral Sciences. *Boston: Cengage Learning.*

Hawks, D. (2014). Equity theory of motivation in management: Definition, examples & quiz. New York: Education Portal.

Hurd, A., Barcelona, R., & Meldrum, J. (2008). *Leisure Services Management.* Champaign: Human Kinetics

Israel, G.D. (2014). *Determining sample size.* Retrieved on December 2, 2014 from http://edis.ifas.ufl.edu/pdffiles/pd/pd00600.pdf

Kalyango, Ronald. (2013). *15 coffee factories closed due to poor handling.* New Vision Kampala.

Karanja, A. M. (1998). Effects of liberalisation measures undertaken in the coffee industry on coffee production, quality and profitability in Kenya. *Kenya Coffee* 63 (743):. 2717-31

Karanja, A. M., & Nyoro, J. K. (2002). Coffee prices and regulation and their impact on livelihoods of rural community in Kenya. *Tegemeo institute of agricultural policy and development, Egerton University*, 27-29.

Karanja, A.M (2002). Liberalisation and smallholder agricultural development. A case
study of coffee farms in Kenya. Ph.D. thesis, Wageningen University. ISBN 90-5808-
603-8.

Kasiulevicius, V., Sapoka, V., & Filipaviciue, R. (2006). *Sample size calculation in epidemiological studies*. Lithuania: Vilnius University.

Kirumba, E.G. & Pinard, F. (2010). *Determinants of farmers' compliance with coffee eco-certification standards in Mt. Kenya region*. Nairobi: World Agro forestry Centre.
http://ageconsearch.umn.edu/bitstream/95970/2/76.%20Coffee%20eco-certification%20in%20Kenya.pdf

Lawler, E. (2000). *Rewarding excellence: Pay strategies for the new economy*. San Francisco,CA: Jossey-Bass.

Lilieholm, Robert J.; W. Paul Weatherly (2010). *"Kibale Forest Wild Coffee: Challenges to Market-Based Conservation in Africa"*. Conservation Biology 24 (4): 924–930.

Livelihoods of rural community in Kenya. Nairobi: Tegemeo Institute of Agricultural Policy and Development.

Mafusire, A., Salami, A., Kamara, A.B., & Lawson, F.E. (2010). The African development bank group chief economist complex. *Commodity market brief*, 1 (2): 2-5

Mitchell, M., & Jolley, J. (2012). Research Design Explained. Boston: Cengage Learning.

Monroy, L., Mulinge, W., & Witwer, M. (2013). *Analysis of incentives and disincentives for coffee in Kenya*. Rome: FAO.

Mugenda, O.M., & Mugenda, A.G. (1999). *Research methods: Quantitative and Qualitative Approaches*. Nairobi: ACTS Press.

Mugenda, O.M., & Mugenda, A.G. (2003). *Research methods: Quantitative and Qualitative Approaches*. Nairobi: ACTS Press.

Mugweru, E. (2011), "Determinants of coffee production in the Kenyan Economy" *university* *of Nairobi*

Mude, A. (2006, August). Weaknesses in institutional organization: explaining the dismal performance of Kenya's coffee cooperatives. In Contributed paper prepared for presentation at the International Association of Agricultural Economists Conference, Gold Coast, Australia.

Mwangome, K. M. (2011). *Impact of the liberalization of coffee marketing rules on the performance of coffee industry in Kenya : a survey of coffee farmers' co-operative socities in Mathira Division, Nyeri District.* Nairobi: Kenyatta University Institutional Repository. http://ir-library.ku.ac.ke/handle/123456789/1045

Nathalie, Johnson. (2002). *"Projects : Kibale Forest Wild Coffee Project.* The World Bank". Washington, DC: World Bank.

Ojambo, F.(2013). *"Uganda Coffee Exports Drop for Second Month as Rains Curb Drying".* Bloomberg.

Okibo, B.W. (2013), Effects of Liberalization on Coffee Production in Kenya. *European Journal of Business and Management*, 5(3), 1-17

Okoth, S. (2013). Policy failures and inadequate technical capacity hurting Kenya's coffee industry. *Business Daily, pp A1-A2.*

Sagor, R. (2000). Data Collection*: Building a Valid and Reliable Data Collection Plan.* Alexandria: Association for Supervision and Curriculum Development.

Scholl, R.W. (2002). Motivation: Expectancy theory. Kingston*: Schmidt Labor Research Center*

Shuttleworth, M. (2008). *Descriptive Research Design.* Retrieved on march 26th 2015 from http://www.experiment-resources.com/descriptive-research-design.html

Sonnentag, S. & Frese, M. (2001). *Performance Concepts and Performance Theory*: Konstanz: University of Konstanz.

Theuri, B. N. (2012), *Factors affecting coffee revitalization Programmes in Mukurweini District Nyeri County, Kenya.* Nairobi: University of Nairobi.

Tomlinson, C.A., Kaplan, S. N., Renzulli, J. S., Purcell, J., Leppien, J., & Burns, D. (2002). *The parallel curriculum: A design to develop high potential and challenge high-ability learners.* Thousand Oaks, CA: Corwin Press.

44

United States Agency for International Development (USAID), (2010). *Kenya coffee industry value chain analysis: profiling the actors, their interactions, costs, constraints and* opportunities. Washington, D.C.: Chemonics International Inc.

Vroom, V.H., Deci, E.L., Penguin (1983). Vroom's expectancy theory. Cambridge: University of Cambridge.

Wangechi R.W. (2010). Factor that Contribute To the Declining Trend of Coffee Production in Kenya: The Case in Nyeri County. Nairobi: *University of Nairobi.*

Werner, s., & Ones, D. S. (2000). Determinants of perceived pay inequities: the effect of comparison other characteristics and pay system communication. *Journal of Applied Social Psychology*, 30(6), 1281-1309.

60761949R00037

Made in the USA
Lexington, KY
18 February 2017